W9-AQD-784

McLEAN MERCER REGIONAL LIBRARY
BOX 505
RIVERDALE, ND 58565

T-BALL

BY KARA L. LAUGHLIN

The Child's World®
childsworld.com

Published by The Child's World®
1980 Lookout Drive • Mankato, MN 56003-1705
800-599-READ • www.childsworld.com

ACKNOWLEDGMENTS
The Child's World®: Mary Swensen, Publishing Director
The Design Lab: Design
Heidi Hogg: Editing
Sarah M. Miller: Editing

PHOTO CREDITS
© Brian Eichhorn/Shutterstock.com: 13; Charles Mann/iStockphoto.com: 9; Chris Hill/Dreamstime.com: 6-7; Daniel Bendjy/iStockphoto.com: 15; Digital Media Pro/Shutterstock.com: cover, 1; Guzel Studio/Shutterstock.com: 2-3; Hurst Photo/Shutterstock.com: 4; RBFried/iStockphoto.com: 19; RonTech2000/iStockphoto.com: 10, 16; Yvonne Chamberlain/iStockphoto.com: 20

COPYRIGHT © 2017 by The Child's World®
All rights reserved. No part of this book may be reproduced or utilized in any form or by any means without written permission from the publisher.

ISBN: 9781503807815
LCCN: 2015958136

Printed in the United States of America
Mankato, MN
June, 2016
PA02300

TABLE OF CONTENTS

Game Time!

Strap on your helmet. Grab your bat. It is time to play T-ball!

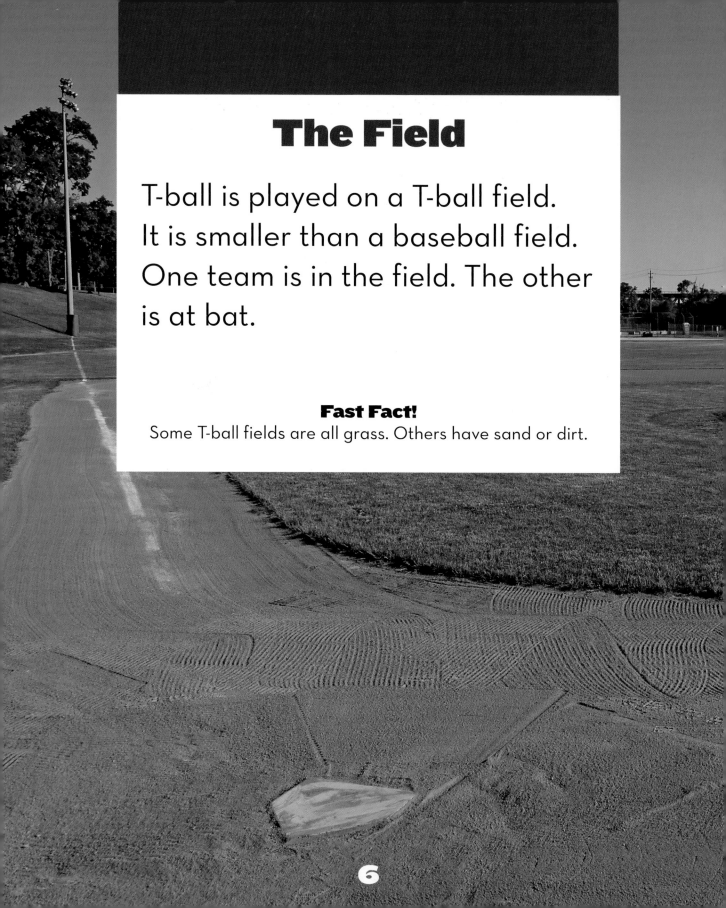

The Field

T-ball is played on a T-ball field. It is smaller than a baseball field. One team is in the field. The other is at bat.

Fast Fact!
Some T-ball fields are all grass. Others have sand or dirt.

The Tee

The ball rests on a **batting tee**. The tee holds the ball still. It is just the right height to swing at.

Fast Fact!
The tee is made of rubber so that it can bend.

Batting

The batter hits the ball! But it rolls to the side. **Foul** ball! That's okay. Each player swings until he hits a **fair** ball.

Fast Fact!
The balls used in T-ball are softer than regular baseballs.

Running the Bases

SMACK! It is a fair ball! The batter runs to first base. Then he waits for the next hit. Each hit is a chance to run to the next base. When a player crosses **home plate**, it is a **run**.

Fast Fact!
Just like in baseball, there are four bases in T-ball.

Everyone on the team has been up to bat. Time to switch sides.

Fast Fact!
Keeping your eye on the ball when you swing is very important.

The Infield

In the **infield**, a player stands at each base. There is also a **pitcher** and a **shortstop**. They try to get the ball to a base before the runner gets there. If they can, that runner is out.

Fast Fact!
It is important to wear good running shoes when playing T-ball.

The Outfield

The rest of the team is in the **outfield**. If the ball pops up in the air, they try to catch it. If they do, it is an out.

Fast Fact!
About 2 million children in the United States play T-ball.

A T-ball game lasts an hour or two. Every player gets to bat two or three times. That way everyone has a chance to have fun!

Fast Fact!
Teams shake hands after each game. It is a way to show other players that you had a good time.

Glossary

batting tee (BAT-ting TEE): A waist-high stick with a base on the bottom and a dent in the top. The ball rests in the dent until a player swings at it.

fair (FAYR): A ball that moves forward far enough to be in play is called fair.

foul (FOWL): A ball that rolls backward after it's hit. The batter cannot run to first base after a foul ball and has to swing again instead.

home plate (HOHM PLAYT): The house-shaped base where the tee stands. Home plate is also the base to cross to earn a run.

infield (IN-feeld): The part of the T-ball field from the bases forward is called the infield.

outfield (OWT-feeld): The outfield is the part of the T-ball field behind the bases.

pitcher (PICH-er): A player who stays near the pitcher's mound and throws to the other infielders is called a pitcher.

run (RUN): A point in T-ball is called a run.

shortstop (SHORT-stop): A shortstop is a player who stays between second and third base.

To Learn More

In the Library

Berenstain, Stan, and Jan Berenstain. *The Berenstain Bears Play T-Ball*. New York, NY: Harper Collins, 2005.

Jacobs, Greg. *The Everything Kids' Baseball Book*. Avon, MA: Adams Media, 2014.

Mara, Will. *Tee Ball*. New York, NY: Children's Press, 2012.

On the Web

Visit our Web site for links about T-ball:
childsworld.com/links

Note to Parents, Teachers, and Librarians: We routinely verify our Web links to make sure they are safe and active sites. So encourage your readers to check them out!

Index

About the Author

Kara L. Laughlin is an artist and writer who lives in Virginia with her husband, three kids, two guinea pigs, and a dog. She is the author of two dozen nonfiction books for kids.

McLEAN MERCER REGIONAL LIBRARY
BOX 505
RIVERDALE, ND 58565